JUST

shakes &
smoothies

KUDOS

Published by Kudos, an imprint of Top That! Publishing plc.

Copyright © 2005 Top That! Publishing plc,

Tide Mill Way, Woodbridge, Suffolk, IP12 IAP.

www.kudosbooks.com

Kudos is a Trademark of Top That! Publishing plc

Contents

Treat your Taste Buds	4
Kitchen Kit	6
Meal in a Glass	8
Fruit Basket	10
Smoothie Store Cupboard	22
Dress your Drink	24

Breakfast Bliss

Cranberry Kiss	26
Grapefruit Blush	28
Raspberry Dream	30
Blueberry Pie	32
Strawberry Sunrise	34
Apricot Ice	36
Vanilla Plum	38
Peach Froth	40

Mango Cream	42
Christmas Cranberry	44

Energy Rush

Blackberry Delight	46
Celery Tonic	48
Melon Thickie	50
Black Forest	52
Carrot Cooler	54
Pear Perfection	56
Italian Tomato	58
Banana Burst	60
Racy Reds	62
Mint Mango	64

Kids' Parties

Strawberry Cookies	66

Black Orange	68	Dark Strawberry	102
Witches' Brew	70	Pineapple Cream	104
Shipwreck	72	Cocktail Hour	
Fairy Froth	74	Tia Tropical	106
Vampire's Breath	76	Tomato Tang	108
Cheeky Monkey	78	Cassis Dream	110
Strawberry Sticks	80	Crimson Crush	112
Mud Pie	82	Kirsch Castaway	114
Banana Big Time	84	Sea Breezer	116
Sinful Sundaes		Mandarin Mirage	118
Hazelnut Heaven	86	Raspberry Cane	120
Almond Ambrosia	88	Pineapple Spice	122
Gooseberry Delight	90	Melon Cooler	124
Raspberry Zest	92	Fruit Index	126
Rhubarb Fool	94	Credits	128
Cherry Pie	96		
Blue Melba	98		
Summer Pudding	100		

Treat your Taste Buds

Smoothies and shakes are a five-minute fix for hunger pangs, packed with vitamins and brimming with fruit. All you need is a bowl full of your favourite fruit – chop, blend and drink!

These recipes are based upon two servings of 350 ml (12 fl oz) liquid to three generous handfuls of fruit, but these are rough guidelines only and recipes will vary.

The beauty of smoothies and shakes is that you can throw in whatever you have to hand and create simple, delicious drinks you're sure to love.

Take your pick from this chilled selection. There are ten recipes for you to try in each section, starting with Breakfast Bliss. For an anytime tonic try one of the Energy Rush pick-me-ups and wind down later with a tipple created from the Cocktail Hour. Kids will love the party recipes, and the desserts in Sinful Sundaes are perfect for solitary indulgence. Enjoy!

Kitchen Kit

Your basic smoothie and shake kit will comprise a sharp knife, a chopping board and a blender. Here are some more kitchen kit suggestions:

Measuring cups and spoons

Most of the recipes use constant volumes, but have a measuring jug and other measuring devices to hand. 250 ml should equate with 9 fl oz, while a teaspoon equals 5 ml and a tablespoon 15 ml.

Long-handled spoons, stirrers and straws

How else will you get to the bottom of the glass?

Smoothie maker

The one pictured here has a handy tap so you can pour your drink straight into the glass, but a blender will do just fine.

Fruit squeezer

Give your recipes that extra zing with a squirt or two of freshly squeezed fruit juice.

Ice cream scoop
You mean you don't have one already?

Ice lolly mould
Frozen smoothies on sticks are a real treat for kids and adults.

Honey spoon
For delving deep into a pot of golden runny honey.

Zester
Pare the rind from citrus fruits and use as a decorative garnish.

Grater
Perfect for adding fresh vegetable ingredients or some fresh root ginger to your drink.

Meal in a Glass

Make the most of your fruity repertoire by serving them in a variety of glasses to do them justice.

Tumbler
Short and sturdy – ideal for thick vegetable drinks.

Goblet
The depth and solid base is perfect for milk shakes.

Cocktail glass
Long-stemmed glasses add a certain finesse to your prepared cocktail.

Decorative glass

Rippled, frosted or decorated glasses can really dress your drink to perfection.

Sundae glass

These are just the right size for a rich and creamy dessert.

Fruit Basket

The following pages give you a listing of the main fruit ingredients used in this book.

It is recommended that you always buy fresh fruit that is in season as it will be readily available and reasonably priced from your local supermarket or grocer. One of the nicest things about making a smoothie is that you can take advantage of the seasonal tastes around you and vary your menu according to the fruit you will see on offer.

Where appropriate, the best varieties have been suggested, as well as when they are in season, and how best to prepare them.

Use your fruit basket to store and ripen fruit so that you always have some fresh at hand.

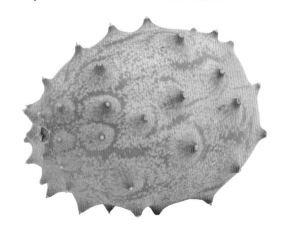

Full of fibre, apples are a good detoxifying ingredient and will help to aid digestion. Peel (if you wish), core and chop. Make them into an apple sauce by cooking them gently on the stove and adding sugar to taste. Apple sauce makes a delicious and healthy addition to a smoothie sundae.

Apple

Select crisp, tart varieties such as Granny Smith, Braeburn, Gala and Discovery. Whilst they are available all year, make the most of a glut of them in autumn from September to November.

Pear

Comice pears, available in winter, make a good smoothie base. Use ripe pears that are scented to touch. Peel, quarter and core.

Banana

Available all year round, bananas are full of fibre and carbohydrates so will give you lots of energy. Over-ripe bananas are perfect for blending into drinks, just slice and blend.

Blackberry

Freely found in autumn hedgerows, blackberries are rich in vitamin C and antioxidants. Wash them well before freezing or blending.

Raspberry

From May to September you'll find raspberries ripe for eating. Pick out and discard any that are mouldy before gently washing the rest. Raspberries can be made into a sauce by simply mashing them with a fork. If you want you can strain them through a sieve to make a pure red pouring sauce that is unbeatable on ice cream.

Lime

Lime juice and zest, bursting with vitamin C, will wake up any drink!

Cherry

Make the most of cherries from June to August when you'll find a glut of them in the shops. To pit cherries, halve and remove the stone with your fingertips. They make an excellent decoration when dipped in chocolate.

Coconut

The addition of coconut milk to any smoothie or shake makes for a creamy-tasting drink that is hard to beat.

Rhubarb

Field rhubarb is in season in April, and the pink stalks make a delicious purée. Pick a bunch that is not stringy or discoloured and slice it into chunks. Cook gently on the stove adding brown sugar to taste. Its tart flavour and thick consistency make this ideal for dolloping on ice cream.

Lemon

A squeeze of fresh lemon juice adds a welcome bite to thick vegetable smoothies. Be creative with the lemon zest shavings as decoration.

Melon

Honeydew or cantaloupe melons are widely available. Pick ripe melons that smell sweet and are tender to touch. Halve them, slice and cut the flesh away from the rind, then chop into chunks.

Mango
April to July is mango season. Pick a mango that is tender to the touch with a sweet smell – especially the amber ones that are really sweet. Peel and slice the creamy flesh into bite-sized chunks and you'll be forgiven for letting the juice drip off your chin!

Blueberry
Sweet and juicy, blueberries are readily available, especially in the summer months. Rich in vitamin C, they give a sweet flavour. Pick fruit that is plump and juicy and not shrivelled in any way.

Grapefruit

From ruby red to pale yellow flesh, grapefruit can be found all year round and make a refreshing addition to drinks. Cut a slice off one end and place, end down, on your chopping board. Cut the peel off leaving the flesh so that you can cut the segments out with a small, serrated knife. Tinned grapefruit in its own juice makes a handy store cupboard standby.

Peach

Peaches are in season in June and July. You should pick velvety-skinned fruit that is unblemished and sweet smelling. Halve and remove the stone with a spoon before dicing.

Orange

Rich in vitamin C, use freshly squeezed or unsweetened orange juice as a base for your drink and save some orange slices for a garnish.

Plum

Plums can be found from May right up until October. Pick ripe ones with a sweet juicy centre, and experiment with different colours ranging from golden, through to green and purple.

Pineapple

Rich in minerals and vitamins, pineapples make an excellent ingredient for smoothies and shakes. Readily available, slice away the top and bottom of the fruit then cut down the sides to remove the skin. Slice and dice the fruit.

Apricot

Fresh apricots are at their best in June and July. Pick fruit that smells sweet and is soft to the touch. Halve and remove the stones.

19

Redcurrant

Use a fork to gently remove the tiny red berries from their stalks, although they also make a pretty garnish complete with stalk.

Blackcurrant

The sharp tang of blackcurrant makes a welcome addition to drinks, and the fruit itself looks gorgeous scattered over a smoothie sundae. These are an excellent source of vitamin C and other antioxidants. Buy blackcurrants (or pick your own) in the summer and freeze for a useful 'forest fruit' addition to drinks.

Cranberry

These bright red berries have a tart flavour and you'll find them in season from October through to December. Cranberry juice is a renowned health drink, excellent for combating urinary tract infections.

Strawberry

Traditionally eaten in June when the strawberry season begins in earnest, make the most of fruit from local suppliers if possible. Nothing beats the taste of home-grown strawberries. Steer clear of mouldy or bruised fruit. Wash well, remove the hulls and save the nicest looking ones for decoration.

Smoothie Store Cupboard

Smoothies are simple to make and your store cupboard needs only a few basic ingredients to keep as useful standbys.

Make it easy on yourself by slicing your fruit up once a week then freezing it flat in self-seal plastic bags. Fresh fruit frozen is good for you and good for the drink, because it will make your drink ice cold and seductively thick. Always keep ice cubes and some ice cream in the freezer. Ensure you have these staple ingredients and you'll be able to whizz up a smoothie or shake any time:

- Fresh fruit in season
- Tinned fruit in its own juice
- Unsweetened fruit or vegetable juice
- Organic live natural yoghurt

- Coconut milk
- Hot pepper/ Worcestershire sauce
- Elderflower cordial
- Mixed spice/cinnamon
- Vanilla/almond essence
- Maple and flavoured syrups
- Vanilla ice cream

Create your own classic combinations by experimenting with the recipes in this book. Have fun!

Dress your Drink

Presentation is everything when you treat your friends to these delicious recipes. Dress your drinks as simply as you wish using different coloured fruit to complement the drink.

You could also try any of these ideas for extra effect...

Chocolate-dipped fruits
Melt some good quality plain chocolate in a basin over a pan of hot water. Dip the fruit and leave to set on a baking sheet lined with non-stick baking paper.

Glass frosting
Rub the glass rim with a wedge of citrus fruit, then dip the glass into the frosting of your choice. It might be sugar, salt, desiccated coconut, ground hazelnuts – you choose!

Citrus curls
Using a zester, pare some strips of citrus rind then sprinkle with caster sugar.

Cranberry Kiss

Serves: 2

Give yourself a kick-start in the morning with this frothy pink delight.

What you need:
- 350 ml cranberry juice
- 3 handfuls strawberries, sliced
- 1 small banana, sliced
- 4 ice cubes, crushed

What you do:
i. Place all the ingredients in a blender and whizz until smooth.
ii. Pour into two glasses.
iii. Drink immediately.

Top tip!
Crush the ice cubes by putting them in a plastic bag, then bash gently with a rolling pin.

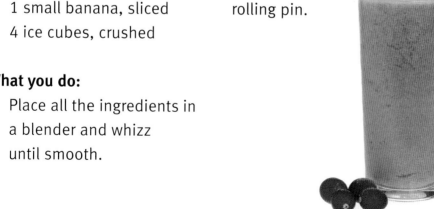

27

Grapefruit Blush

This blend of grapefruit and pineapple is sharp and tangy and makes an excellent wake-up call.

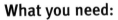

Serves: 2

What you need:

- 350 ml pineapple juice
- 3 handfuls pineapple, chopped
- 240 ml tinned pink grapefruit, drained
- 4 ice cubes, crushed

What you do:

i. Place all the ingredients in a blender and whizz until smooth.
ii. Pour into two glasses.
iii. Drink immediately.

Top tip!
Add a sprinkling of freshly grated root ginger before you blend.

Raspberry Dream

Close your eyes and dream of summer. This is raspberries and cream in a glass.

What you need:
- 350 ml orange juice
- 3 handfuls raspberries
- 1 tbsp good quality, thick natural yoghurt
- 4 ice cubes, crushed

What you do:
i. Place all the ingredients in a blender and whizz until smooth.

ii. Pour into two glasses.

iii. Drink immediately.

Top tip!
Add a drop or two of orange flower water for added flavour before you blend.

Blueberry Pie

Bring this breakfast back to bed with you – it's truly sublime.

What you need:
- 350 ml orange juice
- 3 handfuls blueberries
- 1 small banana, sliced
- 4 ice cubes, crushed

What you do:
i.   Place all the ingredients in a blender and whizz until smooth.
ii. Pour into two glasses.
iii. Drink immediately.

Top tip!
Serve this as a seductive pouring sauce on good quality vanilla ice cream.

Strawberry Sunrise

Watch the sun rise as you sip this heavenly mix of mango and strawberry.

Serves: 2

What you need:

- 350 ml orange juice
- 3 handfuls strawberries, hulled and sliced
- 3 handfuls mango, sliced
- 4 ice cubes, crushed

What you do:

i. Place all the ingredients in a blender and whizz until smooth.
ii. Pour into two glasses.
iii. Drink immediately.

Top tip!

Pick the juiciest, ripest mango you can find and save some for later. Mango is best savoured alone so that you can let the juices of the soft, creamy flesh trickle down your chin.

Apricot Ice

The addition of coconut milk turns this into a dreamy apricot nectar.

What you need
- 350 ml coconut milk
- 1 banana, sliced
- 3–4 handfuls apricot, sliced
- 4 ice cubes, crushed

What you do:
i. Place all the ingredients in a blender and whizz until smooth.

ii. Pour into two glasses.

iii. Drink immediately.

Top tip!
Go easy on the banana as apricots have a delicate flavour that can be easily overshadowed.

Vanilla Plum

A sprinkling of vanilla makes this a soothing start to the day.

Serves: 2

What you need:
- 350 ml apple juice
- 3 handfuls plums, chopped
- 1 tbsp good quality, thick and creamy natural yoghurt
- 4 ice cubes, crushed
- dash of vanilla essence

What you do:
i. Place all the ingredients in a blender and whizz until smooth.
ii. Pour into two glasses.
iii. Drink immediately.

Top tip!
Dark purple plum will give the drink a pleasant speckled effect.

Peach Froth

Brimming with peaches, this frothy drink is bound to put a spring in your step.

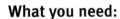

Serves: 2

What you need:
- 350 ml apple juice
- 3 handfuls strawberries, hulled and sliced
- 3 handfuls peaches, stoned and chopped
- 4 ice cubes, crushed

What you do:
i. Place all the ingredients in a blender and whizz until smooth.
ii. Pour into two glasses.
iii. Drink immediately.

Top tip!
Choose peaches that are soft to touch with a heady sweet perfume – these are truly ripe.

Mango Cream

Start your day with the creamy sweetness of mango – you'll be dancing to the office!

Serves: 2

What you need:

- 350 ml orange juice
- 1 small banana, sliced
- 3 handfuls mango, sliced
- 4 ice cubes, crushed

What you do:

i. Place all ingredients in the blender and whizz until smooth.
ii. Pour into two glasses.
iii. Drink immediately.

Top tip!

If making this for a friend, decorate it with a cocktail parasol to complement its sunshine yellow colour.

Christmas Cranberry

Serves: 2

Curl up in front of a log fire with the delicious flavours of cranberry, orange and mixed spice.

What you need:

- 350 ml orange juice
- 3 handfuls cranberries
- 1 tbsp good quality, thick and creamy natural yoghurt
- 4 ice cubes, crushed
- large pinch of mixed spice

What you do:

i. Place all the ingredients in a blender and whizz until smooth.
ii. Pour into two glasses.
iii. Drink immediately.

Top tip!

Add some orange zest or a cinnamon stick as a garnish.

44

Blackberry Delight

An autumnal blend of fresh blackberries and pineapple – this purple smoothie is an excellent pick-me-up any time of the day.

Serves: 2

What you need:

- 350 ml pineapple juice
- 2 handfuls pineapple, chopped
- 3 handfuls blackberries
- 4 ice cubes, crushed

What you do:

i. Place all the ingredients in a blender and whizz until smooth.

ii. Pour into two glasses.

iii. Drink immediately.

Top tip!

Make this when blackberries are in season as the bigger the blackberry, the better the flavour.

Celery Tonic

This crisp, fresh-tasting blend of celery and apple benefits from the extra bite of ginger.

What you need:
- 350 ml apple juice
- 3 handfuls apple, chopped
- 3 handfuls celery, chopped
- 4 ice cubes, crushed
- generous pinch of freshly grated root ginger

What you do:
i. Place all the ingredients in a blender and whizz until smooth.
ii. Pour into two glasses.
iii. Drink immediately.

Top tip!
There's no need to peel the apples first. The apple peel adds to the fibre content of the drink.

Serves: 2

48

Melon Thickie

Sip this refresher in the shade on a hot summer's day.

Serves: 2

What you need:
- 350 ml orange juice
- 3 handfuls mango, sliced
- 3 handfuls melon, chopped
- 3 handfuls pineapple, chopped
- 4 ice cubes, crushed

What you do:
i.   Place all the ingredients in a blender and whizz until smooth.
ii. Pour into two glasses.
iii. Drink immediately.

Top tip!
This is such a refreshing drink, you could pour it straight into ice lolly moulds so that you can enjoy it frozen as well.

Black Forest

Forest fruits are the perfect addition to this honey-laced smoothie.

Serves: 2

What you need:
- 350 ml orange juice
- 3 handfuls forest fruits (blackcurrants, blueberries, black cherries, blackberries)
- 1 tbsp good quality, thick natural yoghurt
- 1 generous spoonful of runny honey
- 4 ice cubes, crushed

What you do:
i. Place all the ingredients in a blender and whizz until smooth.
ii. Pour into two glasses.
iii. Drink immediately.

Top tip!
Add some sprigs of fresh mint leaves to garnish.

Carrot Cooler

This fantastic orange creation makes a perfect lunchtime drink.

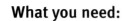

Serves: 2

What you need:

- 350 ml orange juice
- 3 handfuls carrot, peeled and grated
- 4 ice cubes, crushed

What you do:

i. Place all the ingredients in a blender and whizz until smooth.

ii. Pour into two glasses.

iii. Drink immediately.

Top tip!
Add a pinch or two of cinnamon before blending.

Pear Perfection

If you like fruit pies, you'll love this pie in a glass.

Serves: 2

What you need:

- 350 ml apple juice
- 3 handfuls pear, chopped
- 3 handfuls blackberries
- 4 ice cubes, crushed

What you do:

i.   Place all the ingredients in a blender and whizz until smooth.
ii. Pour into two glasses.
iii. Drink immediately.

Top tip!

Decorate this with a swirl of double cream and drink it through a straw.

Italian Tomato

The mix of tomatoes and orange make this a vital vitamin drink to pep you up when your energy levels are flagging.

 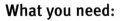

What you need:

- 350 ml orange juice
- 3 handfuls tomato, chopped
- squeeze of fresh lemon juice
- 1 handful fresh basil leaves, roughly torn
- sea salt and freshly ground black pepper to taste
- 4 ice cubes, crushed

What you do:

i. Place all the ingredients in a blender and whizz until smooth.
ii. Pour into two glasses.
iii. Drink immediately.

Top tip!

Tearing the basil leaves makes the most of the fresh flavour – so keep the chopping knife in the draw!

Banana Burst

Next time you fancy a hot curry, make this your refreshing drink on the side. It's sure to cool down that hot and spicy aftertaste.

Serves: 2

What you need:

- 350 ml coconut milk
- 2 bananas, sliced
- large dash of maple syrup
- 4 ice cubes, crushed

What you do:

i. Place all the ingredients in a blender and whizz until smooth.
ii. Pour into two glasses.
iii. Drink immediately.

Top tip!

If you're serving this to friends, decorate the glass with a frosting of coconut first.

Racy Reds

This magenta mix is the ideal drink to savour for a mid-morning snack.

What you need:
- 350 ml orange juice
- 3 handfuls red fruits (cherries, redcurrants, raspberries, strawberries)
- 240 ml tinned pink grapefruit, drained
- 4 ice cubes, crushed

What you do:
i.   Place all the ingredients in a blender and whizz until smooth.
ii. Pour into two glasses.
iii. Drink immediately.

Top tip!
Use a mixture of fresh and frozen fruit, depending on what's in season.

Mint Mango

Drink this invigorating blend of mango and mint at lunchtime to set you up for the afternoon.

Serves: 2

What you need:
- 4 handfuls mango, sliced
- 3 tbsp good quality, thick natural yoghurt
- 2 tbsp runny honey
- 1 squeeze fresh lime juice
- pinch freshly chopped mint
- 4 ice cubes, crushed

What you do:
i. Place all the ingredients in a blender and whizz until smooth.
ii. Pour into two glasses.
iii. Drink immediately.

Top tip!
Fresh mint has a very distinctive flavour. Use it sparingly or it will overshadow the mango taste.

Strawberry Cookies

Serves: 2

Kids will find this mixture of chocolate chip cookies and strawberries simply irresistible. Make it for a summer party treat.

What you need:

- 2 handfuls chocolate chip cookies, crumbled
- 3 handfuls strawberries, hulled and sliced
- 350 ml creamy strawberry yoghurt
- 4 ice cubes, crushed

What you do:

i.   Place all the ingredients in a blender and whizz until smooth.
ii. Pour into two glasses.
iii. Serve immediately.

Top tip!

Add a chocolate flake as a stirrer and for reaching the bottom of the glass.

Black Orange

Since eleven-year-old American Frank Epperson first invented the 'Epsicle' (later known as the 'popsicle') in 1905, the ice lolly has fast become a finger food favourite for kids.

Serves: 2

What you need:
- 3 handfuls blackcurrants
- 240 ml orange juice
- caster sugar

What you do:
i.   Cook the blackcurrants gently in a little water over a low heat.

ii. Sweeten to taste with caster sugar and leave to cool.

iii. Press the purée through a sieve with the back of a large spoon and fill half the lolly mould.

iv. Freeze until hard.

v.   Pour in the orange juice layer so that the mould is full.

vi. Freeze until hard.

Top tip!
If you don't have lolly moulds, you can use empty yoghurt pots or deep ice cube trays.

Witches' Brew

Trick or treaters will love this mint milkshake drink on Hallowe'en.

Serves: 2

What you need:
- 350 ml milk
- 4 scoops mint ice cream
- 2 drops green food colouring

What you do:
i. Place all the ingredients in a blender and whizz until smooth.
ii. Pour into two glasses.
iii. Serve immediately.

Top tip!
Decorate with 'bats' eyeballs' (redcurrants or blackcurrants).

Shipwreck

Serves: 2

No pirate party would be complete without glasses of 'Shipwreck' – the tropical milk shake of the day.

What you need:

- 350 ml milk
- 350 ml pineapple yoghurt
- 3 handfuls pineapple, chopped
- 3 scoops vanilla ice cream

What you do:

i. Place all the ingredients in a blender and whizz until smooth.
ii. Pour into two glasses.
iii. Serve immediately.

Top tip!

Serve with 'pirate's treasure' – coconut shells filled with tiny sweets.

Fairy Froth

This sweet and sparkly ice cream soda is perfect for parties with a pink theme.

What you need:

- 350 ml cherry soda
- 4 scoops vanilla ice cream

What you do:

i.   Place all the ingredients in a blender and whizz until smooth.
ii. Pour into two glasses.
iii. Serve immediately.

Top tip!

Drizzle strawberry syrup over the top like a fairy necklace, and make sure there are enough magic wands to go round.

Vampire's Breath

Serves: 2

This frothy blackcurrant drink should be served in extra cold glasses straight from the vampire's vault.

What you need:

- 350 ml cola
- dash of blackcurrant cordial
- 1 handful blackcurrants (or forest fruits)
- 3 scoops vanilla ice cream

What you do:

i. Place all the ingredients in a blender and whizz until smooth.
ii. Pour into two glasses.
iii. Serve immediately.

Top tip!

Decorate with 'fang chippings' (desiccated coconut).

Cheeky Monkey

Serves:

This peanut butter and banana concoction is delicious. Kids won't want to wait for a party to drink it.

What you need:
- 350 ml milk
- dash chocolate syrup
- 1 generous tbsp peanut butter
- 1 banana, sliced
- 3 scoops vanilla ice cream

What you do:
i. Place all the ingredients in a blender and whizz until smooth.
ii. Pour into two glasses.
iii. Serve immediately.

WARNING!
Contains nuts.

Strawberry Sticks

Sometimes the simplest recipes of all are still the best...

Serves: 2

What you need:
- 350 ml milk
- 2 teaspoons strawberry milkshake powder

What you do:
i. Mix the strawberry powder into the milk.
ii. Pour into the lolly moulds and freeze until firm.

Top tip!
Use full-fat milk which is ideal for small children.

Mud Pie

Make this chocolate milkshake as muddy as you like with a combination of favourite chocolate flavours.

Serves: 2

What you need:
- 4 scoops chocolate ice cream
- 350 ml milk
- dash chocolate syrup

What you do:
i. Place all the ingredients in a blender and whizz until smooth.
ii. Pour into two glasses.
iii. Serve immediately.

Top tip!
Crumble or grate some chocolate on top and create a muddy puddle topping.

Banana Big Time

Serves: 2

Blended with apricots and frothed with ice cream, this is the mother of all milkshakes.

What you need:

- 3 handfuls apricots, chopped
- 1 large banana, sliced
- 2 tbsp apricot jam
- 4 scoops vanilla ice cream
- 350 ml milk

What you do:

i. Place the apricots, banana and jam in a blender and whizz into a smooth purée.

ii. Add two scoops of ice cream. Keep the blender running, gradually adding the milk until frothy. Pour into two glasses.

iii. Add another scoop of ice cream to each glass and serve immediately.

Top tip!
Tinned apricots are ideal in this rich and creamy shake.

Hazelnut Heaven

Serves: 1

Raspberries and hazelnuts blended together make a heavenly combination that's hard to beat.

What you need:

- 2 handfuls raspberries
- 1 scoop vanilla ice cream
- 120 ml double cream
- 2 tbsp hazelnut flavour syrup

What you do:

i.   Place all the ingredients in a blender and whizz until smooth.
ii. Pour into a glass.
iii. Indulge yourself.

Top tip!

Decorate with roasted, chopped hazelnuts to complement the delicious nutty taste.

WARNING! Contains nuts.

Almond Ambrosia

Apricots and almonds are made for each other. You can make this when apricots are not in season – tinned ones work just as well.

Serves: 1

What you need:
- 2 handfuls apricots, sliced
- 1 scoop vanilla ice cream
- 120 ml double cream
- 3 or 4 amaretti biscuits, crumbled
- 1 drop almond essence

What you do:
i.   Place all the ingredients in a blender and whizz until smooth.
ii. Pour into a glass.
iii. Indulge yourself.

Top tip!
Decorate with a fine layer of crumbled amaretti biscuits.

Gooseberry Delight

Serves: 1

Elderflower is a natural, accompaniment to gooseberries, making this a delicious summer treat.

What you need:
- 2 handfuls gooseberries
- 2 tbsp elderflower cordial
- 120 ml double cream
- 1 scoop vanilla ice cream

What you do:
i.   Place all the ingredients in a blender and whizz until smooth.
ii. Pour into a glass.
iii. Indulge yourself.

Top tip!
Decorate with cape gooseberries or some fresh elderflowers.

Raspberry Zest

Lemon and raspberry make a perfect partnership that's sure to lift your spirits.

Serves: 1

What you need:
- 2 handfuls raspberries
- 1 tbsp good quality lemon curd
- 120 ml double cream
- 1 scoop raspberry ripple ice cream

What you do:
i.   Place all the ingredients in a blender and whizz until smooth.
ii. Pour into a glass.
iii. Indulge yourself.

Top tip!
Serve with lemon shortbread.

Rhubarb Fool

This is a delicious dessert with a zingy ginger aftertaste.

Serves: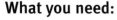

What you need:
- 480 ml rhubarb compote
- 2 tbsp ginger cordial
- 120 ml double cream
- 1 scoop vanilla ice cream

What you do:
i.   Place all the ingredients in a blender and whizz until smooth.
ii. Pour into a glass.
iii. Indulge yourself.

Top tip!
Make your own rhubarb compote by gently cooking some fresh rhubarb in a little cold water and sweeten to taste. Leave until cold. Pink rhubarb will give your dessert a more dreamy colour.

Cherry Pie

A perfect heady mix of creamy coconut milk and plump, ripe cherries.

Serves: 1

What you need:

- 2 handfuls cherries, pitted
- 1 scoop cherry and vanilla ice cream
- 120 ml double cream
- 120 ml coconut milk

What you do:

i.   Place all the ingredients in a blender and whizz until smooth.
ii. Pour into a glass.
iii. Indulge yourself.

Top tip!
Sprinkle a fine layer of desiccated coconut on the top.

Blue Melba

Try this variation on a peach melba theme by replacing the raspberries with blueberries.

What you need:
- 2 handfuls peaches, sliced
- 1 handful blueberries
- splash of orange flower water
- 120 ml double cream
- 1 scoop vanilla ice cream

What you do:
i. Place all the ingredients in a blender and whizz until smooth.
ii. Pour into a glass.
iii. Indulge yourself.

Top tip!
Decorate with sugar frosted blueberries.

Summer Pudding

If you don't have time to make a real summer pudding, this blended version is just as delicious.

Serves: 1

What you need:

- 2 handfuls summer fruits (redcurrants, blackcurrants, raspberries)
- 120 ml double cream
- 1 scoop vanilla ice cream

What you do:

i. Place all the ingredients in a blender and whizz until smooth.

ii. Pour into a glass.

iii. Indulge yourself.

Top tip!

Decorate with a scattering of blackcurrants.

Dark Strawberry

Dark chocolate and rose water are the perfect accompaniment to fresh strawberries.

What you need:
- 2 handfuls strawberries, hulled and sliced
- 1 scoop chocolate ice cream
- 120 ml double cream
- splash of rose water

What you do:
i. Place all the ingredients in a blender and whizz until smooth.
ii. Pour into a glass.
iii. Indulge yourself.

Top tip!
If you prefer, add a dash of chocolate essence instead of the rose water.

Pineapple Cream

Transport yourself to the tropics with this heavenly dessert of mango and pineapple.

Serves: 1

What you need:
- 2 handfuls pineapple, sliced and chopped
- 1 handful mango, sliced
- 120 ml double cream
- 1 scoop vanilla ice cream

What you do:
i. Place all the ingredients in a blender and whizz until smooth.
ii. Pour into a glass.
iii. Indulge yourself.

Top tip!
Serve with a brandy snap to add a contrasting crunch and flavour.

Tia Tropical

This delicious mix of truly tropical tastes should be sipped in a hammock on a hot summer's day.

What you need:
- 350 ml coconut milk
- 1 tbsp rum
- 2 tbsp coffee liqueur
- 2 small bananas, sliced
- 4 ice cubes, crushed

Serves: 2

What you do:

i. Place all the ingredients in a blender and whizz until smooth.

ii. Pour into two glasses.

iii. Serve immediately.

Top tip!

Make sure you have enough ingredients to make a second helping.

107

Tomato Tang

This variation of a traditional Bloody Mary is all the better for the fresh tomato taste.

Serves: 2

What you need:
- juice of half a lime
- 80 ml vodka
- 3 handfuls tomatoes, seeded and chopped
- salt and pepper
- dash of hot pepper, or Worcestershire, sauce
- 4 ice cubes, crushed

What you do:
i.   Place all the ingredients in a blender and whizz until smooth.
ii. Pour into two glasses.
iii. Serve immediately.

Top tip!
Add a pinch of lime zest or freshly chopped coriander for an added kick.

Cassis Dream

Drown in the taste of blackcurrants, and sip this while you slip into something more comfortable.

Serves: 2

What you need:

- 350 ml apple juice
- 3 handfuls blackcurrants
- 60 ml crème de cassis
- 4 ice cubes, crushed

What you do:

i.   Place all the ingredients in a blender and whizz until smooth.
ii. Pour into two glasses.
iii. Serve immediately.

Top tip!

Add some vodka if you prefer a more alcoholic cocktail.

Crimson Crush

This crimson concoction is deliciously refreshing and bursting with fresh strawberry flavour.

What you need:

- 60 ml gin
- 60 ml grenadine
- 3 handfuls strawberries, hulled and sliced
- 4 ice cubes, crushed

What you do:

i.   Place all the ingredients in a blender and whizz until smooth.
ii. Pour into two glasses.
iii. Serve immediately.

Top tip!

Serve in an elegant cocktail glass with a wedge of fresh strawberry.

Serves: 2

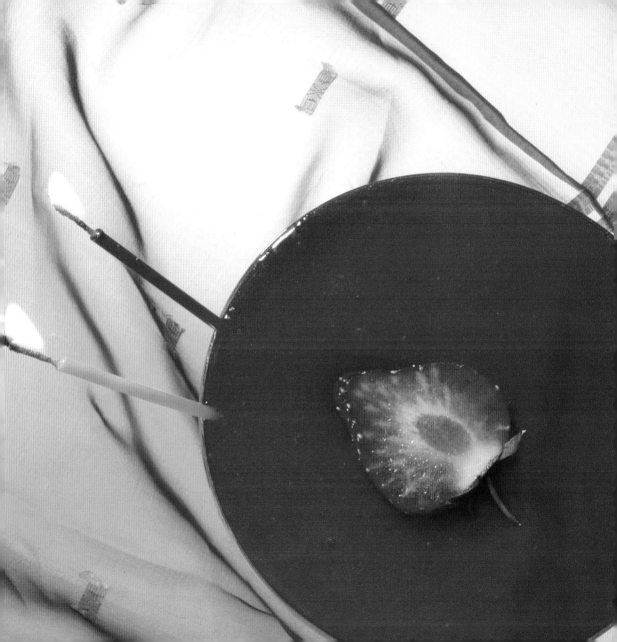

Kirsch Castaway

Serves: 2

Cherry brandy and peaches make an original and refreshing tipple.

What you need:
- 1 tbsp kirsch
- 3 handfuls peaches, sliced
- 120 ml pineapple juice
- 4 ice cubes, crushed

What you do:
i. Place all the ingredients in a blender and whizz until smooth.
ii. Pour into two glasses.
iii. Serve immediately.

Top tip!
Decorate with fresh cherries if they are in season. Or add kitsch kirsch appeal with some bright red cocktail cherries.

Sea Breezer

This frothy concoction tastes quite sharp and is as refreshing as a bracing sea breeze.

Serves: 2

What you need:
- 350 ml cranberry juice
- 3 handfuls grapefruit, sliced
- 80 ml vodka
- 4 ice cubes, crushed

What you do:
i. Place all the ingredients in a blender and whizz until smooth.

ii. Pour into two glasses.

iii. Serve immediately.

Top tip!
Decorate with a pretty pink cocktail parasol and plump ruddy fruit.

Mandarin Mirage

Serves: 2

Mandarin liqueur gives a fragrant orange flavour. If you don't have any to hand any orange flavoured liqueur will do just as nicely.

What you need:
- 480 ml orange juice
- 3 handfuls cranberries
- 1 tbsp mandarin orange liqueur
- 4 ice cubes, crushed

What you do:
i.   Place all the ingredients in a blender and whizz until smooth.
ii. Pour into two glasses.
iii. Serve immediately.

Top tip!
Serve with slices of fresh orange.

Raspberry Cane

Pink, sweet and frothy – perfect for a Valentine's Day evening.

Serves: 2

What you need:
- 480 ml apple juice
- 3 handfuls raspberries
- 60 ml crème de framboise
- 4 ice cubes, crushed

What you do:
i. Place all the ingredients in a blender and whizz until smooth.
ii. Pour into two glasses.
iii. Serve immediately.

Top tip!
Garnish with fresh mint leaves that complement the raspberry colour.

Pineapple Spice

Serves: 2

Treat yourself to this when you return home from work. It'll wake up your flagging energy levels.

What you need:

- 480 ml apple juice
- 1 tbsp rum
- 3 handfuls pineapple, sliced and chopped
- 4 ice cubes, crushed
- sprinkle of fresh root ginger, grated

What you do:

i.   Place all the ingredients in a blender and whizz until smooth.
ii. Pour into two glasses.
iii. Serve immediately.

Top tip!

Fresh pineapple gives this cocktail a really tasty zing.

Melon Cooler

Cool down after a hard day with this soothing thirst quencher.

Serves: 2

What you need:
- 350 ml orange juice
- 3 handfuls melon, sliced
- 60 ml cup gin
- 4 ice cubes, crushed

What you do:
i. Place all the ingredients in a blender and whizz until smooth.
ii. Pour into two glasses.
iii. Serve immediately.

Top tip!
Honeydew melon works well and gives the drink a calming yellow colour.

Fruit Index

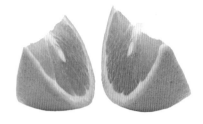

Apple
Celery Tonic 48
Apricot
Apricot Ice 36
Banana Big Time 84
Almond Ambrosia 88
Banana
Cranberry Kiss 26
Blueberry Pie 32
Apricot Ice 36
Mango Cream 42
Banana Burst 60
Cheeky Monkey 78
Banana Big Time 84
Tia Tropical 106

Blackberry
Blackberry Delight 46
Pear Perfection 56
Blackcurrant
Black Orange 68
Vampire's Breath 76
Cassis Dream 110
Blueberry
Blueberry Pie 32
Blue Melba 98
Carrot
Carrot Cooler 54
Celery
Celery Tonic 48

Cherry
Cherry Pie 96
Cranberry
Christmas Cranberry 44
Mandarin Mirage 118
Forest Fruit
Black Forest 52
Gooseberry
Gooseberry Delight 90
Grapefruit
Grapefruit Blush 28
Racy Reds 62
Sea Breezer 116

Mango

Strawberry Sunrise 34

Mango Cream 42

Melon Thickie 50

Mint Mango 64

Pineapple Cream 104

Melon

Melon Thickie 50

Melon Cooler 124

Peach

Peach Froth 40

Blue Melba 98

Kirsch Castaway 114

Pear

Pear Perfection 56

Pineapple

Grapefruit Blush 28

Blackberry Delight 46

Melon Thickie 50

Shipwreck 72

Pineapple Cream 104

Pineapple Spice 122

Plum

Vanilla Plum 38

Raspberry

Raspberry Dream 30

Hazelnut Heaven 86

Raspberry Zest 92

Raspberry Cane 120

Red Fruit

Racy Reds 62

Rhubarb

Rhubarb Fool 94

Strawberry

Cranberry Kiss 26

Strawberry Sunrise 34

Peach Froth 40

Strawberry Cookies 66

Dark Strawberry 102

Crimson Crush 112

Summer Fruit

Summer Pudding 100

Tomato

Italian Tomato 58

Tomato Tang 108

Credits

The author and publisher would like to thank the following for their help in the creation of this book:

Kenwood UK, New Lane, Havant, Hampshire, PO9 2NH, (tel: + 44 (0) 23 9247 6000), for the kind donation of the Kenwood Smoothie Maker. www.kenwood.co.uk

The Woodbridge Kitchen Company, 7, The Thoroughfare, Woodbridge, Suffolk, IP12 1AA (tel: + 44 (0) 394 382 091), for the kind loan of various glasses used in the photography.